D1446463

Praise for
I HEARD YOUR DOG DIED

"An inspiring and charming story filled with healing and spiritual wisdom. I highly recommend this helpful book for anyone who is recovering from a loss."

TRUDY GRISWOLD, AUTHOR OF *ANGELSPEAKE*

✳

"Grief for a beloved pet is just as significant as the loss of any dear friend . . . . Here indeed is a great treasure to help you through the difficult days after the death of a close animal friend."

DR. C. NORMAN SHEALY,
HOLISTIC PAIN AND DEPRESSION SPECIALIST

✳

"There are bereavement storybooks for young children and . . . detailed books for grieving adults, but not many books for people between. The imaginings in this book . . . fill the gap and soothe heartache in a way not previously written about."

DR. KAREN SHAW BECKER, DVM

✳

"This book presents a unique approach to the death of a pet (or anyone else) from a strong cognitive perspective which balances emotions at the same time. Using this process to look at death from a very active and specific frame of reference promotes the transformation of strong and heavy emotions into sweet, warm, uplifting and loving memories in a moment's time . . . .this is a very valuable resource for all those who grieve deeply . . . which may very well be all of us."

DORY DZINSKI, LICENSED PROFESSIONAL COUNSELOR,
TRAUMA DEBRIEFER

I HEARD
YOUR
DOG
DIED

I HEARD YOUR DOG DIED

IMAGININGS FOR THOSE WHO HAVE LOST A PET

BONNIE KREITLER

With dog illustrations by Carole Ohl

RAMBLING DOG PUBLICATIONS
Southport, Connecticut

Rambling Dog Publications LLC
P.O. Box 547
Southport, CT 06890
www.ramblingdogpublications.com

Quote from *The Minpins* by Roald Dahl, copyright © 1991 by Roald Dahl Nominee Limited. Used by permission of Viking Children's Books, an imprint of Penguin Young Readers Group, a division of Penguin Random House LLC in the USA; and by permission of David Higham Associates Limited in the UK.

ISBN 978-0-9970653-7-4

Dog Illustrations by Carole Ohl
Editiorial by Robin Quinn
Book design by Tricia Breidenthal

Names:	Kreitler, Bonnie, author.
Title:	I heard your dog died: imaginings for those who have lost a pet / Bonnie Kreitler.
Description:	First printed edition.	Southport, CT : Rambling Dog Publications, [2016]	Summary: When a youngster's dog dies tragically, a caring neighbor helps the youngster shift from despair to hope by offering fresh perspectives on animal souls, dying, and ways to work through grief.. --Publisher.
Identifiers:	ISBN: 978-0-9970653-7-4	LCCN: 2016940229
Subjects:	LCSH: Dogs--Death--Fiction.	Pets--Death--Fiction.	Dogs—Death— Psychological aspects--Fiction.| Pets--Death----Psychological aspects— Fiction.	Dog owners--Psychology--Fiction.	Pet owners--Psy-chology- -Fiction.	Bereavement--Psychological aspects--Fiction.	Children and death--Fiction.	Grief in children--Fiction.	Human-animal r e l a t i o n - ships—Fiction	CYAC: Dogs--Death--Fiction.	Pets--Death-- Fiction.	Pet owners--Fiction.	Bereavement in children--Fiction.	Children and death--Fiction.	Grief in children--Fiction.	Human- animal re-lationships--Fiction.| BISAC: FICTION / Visionary & Metaphysical.	YOUNG ADULT FICTION / Animals / Pets.	PSYCHOLOGY / Grief & Loss.
Classification:	LCC: PS3611.R445 I44 2016	DDC: 813/.6--dc23

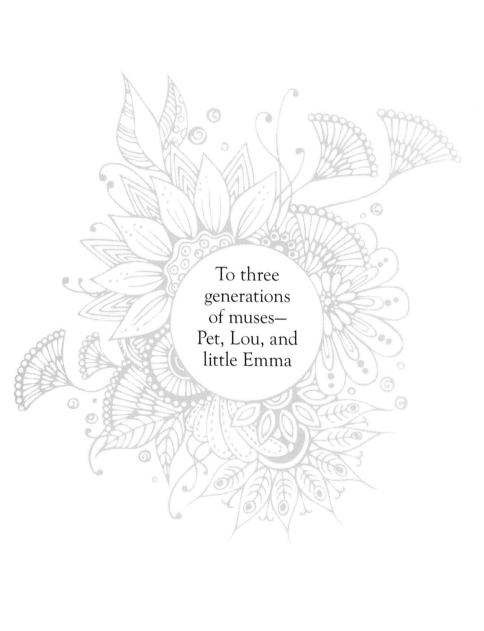

To three
generations
of muses—
Pet, Lou, and
little Emma

CONTENTS

And above all,
watch with glittering eyes
the whole world around you
because the greatest secrets are always hidden
in the most unlikely places.
Those who don't believe in magic will never find it.

ROALD DAHL
THE MINPINS

AUTHOR'S NOTE

This story is for anyone suffering because they've lost a pet.

This story is for grown-ups whose ability to shift effortlessly among an amazing array of imaginative perspectives as they play in the universe may be dulled by time. And no longer children themselves, they can't imagine how to soothe a child navigating the seething emotions in them and around them when a beloved pet's life on earth is over.

This story is for kids who are confused by all sorts of things (very serious things, judging by how the grown-ups are acting) going on around them when any death occurs. Their radar is up. They are watching and listening. And they feel like helpless actors in a Big Play. They don't know where to stand or when to say what or how to contemplate the "why" of it all when their pet dies.

This story unfolds through dialogue alone. I leave it to readers to imagine the child and the adult (even their genders and names, except for the dogs) in ways that conjure their own experiences of living, loving and dying.

Losses are one of humanity's common denominators. They test, they teach, but they need not be tragedies. This story brings generations together to talk, to question, to cry, to clap, to keep love sparks cycling through their lives.

Blessings on all who find this story in their hands.

Bonnie Kreitler

CHAPTER 1

LISTENING

Hi. My mom sent me over with this mail. It's yours but we got it by mistake.

Did you hear? About the accident?

I wasn't home over the weekend when it happened but Mrs. Gordon called last night to tell me about it. I heard your dog died. I'm so very sorry.

Thanks. I'm trying not to cry too much because it makes Mom sad again, too, and she starts crying again. But it's hard. I miss my dog so much.

Well, it's certainly OK for kids or grown-ups to cry when they lose a pet. A best buddy. In fact, it's pretty normal. Would you like to sit here on the steps and tell me what happened?

Somebody left the gate open. He ran into the street in front of a car. It hit him. I heard it hit him! He was just lying there in the street. He didn't move. And the lady driving the car was screaming.

I ran out of the yard but Mrs. Downing grabbed me and wouldn't let me go out in the street to get him. I know I could have helped him! Maybe I could have saved him! My dad went out and picked him up and I never saw my dog again. He's just gone.

I miss him so much.

I know how that feels. You loved him a lot and it always hurts to lose someone you loved. I remember how excited you were when he came as a puppy. What made your dog special to you? What do you miss about him?

I miss the way he was so wiggly and happy when I came home from school.

It's hard when your special buddy isn't there to greet you.

Yeah. And I miss his doggy kisses and even his smelly doggy breath. I miss cuddling with him and using him as a pillow when we watched TV.

Did you and your dog sleep together?

He stayed in my room at night to keep me company. Sometimes I snuck him into my bed, but Mom didn't like that. I always felt safe when my dog was with me.

I feel that way about my dog, too.

When I came home from school today, I just got so sad because he's not there. I feel just . . . alone. And I miss the way my dog always loved me, even if I did something bad. He never yelled at me or gave me a time-out, no matter what.

Ah. You have a lot of reasons to miss him. Dogs have a way of making us feel like the most important person in the world. They make us feel good about ourselves. It's hard to lose that kind of friend.

Yeah. I can't believe he's gone and I'll never see him again! Or snuggle with him again. I'm glad I came over. I feel a little better talking about my dog.

Did you ever have a dog that died?

Oh, I've known and lost quite a few dogs. And other animals, too. I grew up on a farm and I saw many animals born and many die. There's a cycle of coming and going to life. Like the way some plants pop out of the ground when it warms up come spring, grow into flowers come summer, then scatter a bunch of seeds in fall before they hibernate in the ground for winter all over again. Comings and goings.

Your dog died very suddenly. And that's really hard. But the truth is, all dogs have shorter lives than people. Even dogs that get to grow really old, for a dog. I know my Sammy will probably die before I do. But that doesn't keep me from being happy about having her in my life.

Actually, I don't really like the feel of the words "die" or "dead." They just don't seem to describe all the comings and goings of the animals in my life just right.

What do you mean?

Well, "die" and "dead" seem to say that everything about an animal is just "gone" when it stops breathing. Nothing is left. As if they were just a bag of skin and bones. But that never seemed to be the whole story to me, especially when I was your age. I thought about it really hard when I lost my first dog. And then a very kind neighbor by the name of Miss Elaine showed me a way to see things a bit differently. She helped me imagine my dog in a story that made me feel a little better. Over the years I've remembered that story, even imagined it working different ways. I've added to the story quite a bit, come to think of it.

What is it? Can you tell me the story?

Hmmm. I don't tell the story to everyone. I'm really careful about telling it to some people.

Why?

Well, a lot of people, particularly grown-ups, have pretty set ideas about what "die" and "dead" mean. And if your ideas and their ideas aren't the same, they get upset.

Set and upset. That's funny! Why do they get upset by a story?

I'm not sure why. To understand the story, you have to be able to imagine. And some grown-ups have a hard time using their imaginations the way they could when they were little. If you can't imagine, it's hard to see things any other way than the way you already see them. So, they hang on to believing whatever it is they believe about dogs or people being dead, even if it keeps them stuck in being miserable and sad.

Won't you be sad when Sammy dies?

Oh, I'll really miss Sammy when she goes, just like you miss your dog now. Only I don't think of "dead" as "gone forever" anymore. I'll be sad for a while, that's just normal. But I won't stay stuck in being sad forever.

Miss Elaine's story helped me imagine there was a part of my first dog that was still around. And she showed me a way to connect with that part. And feeling I could still connect in some way with my dog made me a little less sad.

You mean like a ghost?

No, not a ghost. More like . . . an imaginary friend. Or like the stuffed animals you play with and talk to and they talk back to you and together you make up little stories you act out and have fun with.

What was the story she told you? Can you tell it to me?

I wonder. Are you too old to understand?

That's a funny thing to say! My mom sometimes tells me I'm too young to understand things. So how can I be too old to understand?

To understand the story, you have to use your imagination. Can you still imagine? Can you imagine that maybe, just maybe, your dog had an invisible "love spark," something that made him a special dog, a particular dog, not just any old dog?

You mean like a soul?

Well, you could call it that if you like. But there we go again. Soul, spirit, ghost . . . those words mean different things to different people. So the way you use those words can agitate some people.

What do you mean?

I mean that if someone doesn't agree with you about exactly what those words mean, they get all bothered, they want to argue about the story instead of listening to it. Soul, spirit, ghost, being! I'm very careful with those words. They mean so many different things to different people that it's hard to know exactly what they do or might mean to somebody else.

I only know that it seems to me that there's some kind of "spark"—something like the electricity that runs through the walls in our houses and lights up light bulbs—that seems to make the difference between being alive and being dead. We can't see it but we can tell when it's there and when it's not.

When the spark was there, your dog could run and jump, bark and wag, give kisses and all that stuff. And when your dog's heart stopped beating and his lungs stopped breathing, the spark went away. Like flipping a light switch off. His body didn't move around anymore. Or maybe it's the other way around. First the spark goes away and then the heart and all that stuff stops. I'm not sure. Doesn't matter.

Either way, your dog's body wasn't alive anymore when the car flipped his switch and his spark left. Something that had been there before, something that made him alive, was gone.

That spark gave him his own personality, things that made him different from other dogs, but something even more than that. Something that animated him and made him different from, say, a rock.

You mean like the way he always followed me everywhere when I was home?

And the way he wagged his tail so hard it hurt when he hit me with it?

And the way he was crazy for chasing balls and swimming?

And ice cream! He loved ice cream so much he snatched a whole cone out of my hand once! Boy, was I mad!

Yes, like that. And can you imagine that his spark didn't stop being him just because his body stopped moving? Can you imagine what your dog's spark might be doing if it was still around, even though you couldn't see it or feel it or hear it?

I think so. I want to. I could try.

Well, then. Maybe you're young enough to hear the story.

CHAPTER 2

ALL THE WORLD
A STAGE

Over time, I've come to call the story "the Big Play." But before I tell you how I imagine the Big Play, I'll tell you the story about how I heard of it in the first place.

My grandpa lived on the farm with us. When I was a bit younger than you, he died. He was pretty old and one day he got sick. After that, he stayed in bed for a long time and my mother took care of him. Then one day I came home from a friend's house and he was just gone. He'd left. Never told me where he was going or if he was coming back.

My mother said he wasn't coming back. She kept saying things I didn't understand, like "It was expected" or "It was his time." Gradually I came to understand that I would never get to ride on the tractor with him ever again, or go fishing, or go into town with him to get ice cream and some library books. He used to say we were tight, we were buddies.

A lot of grown-ups came to the house. They said more things I couldn't understand, like "He passed," or "He's gone to his reward," or "We'll meet him again in heaven," or "He's with the angels." None of what they said helped me figure out where he had gone at all. One old guy said, "He bought the farm" and a lot of people smiled and seemed to think that was a good thing to say.

Why could it be good if he died?

Well, it's something people sometimes say when someone dies. But back then, just like you, it made no sense that saying some things made them sad and saying other things made them smile. None of the things they said to try to make me feel better made me feel better at all. They just reminded me that Grandpa was gone. I'd never sit in his lap again or get a quarter that he'd pulled from behind my ear.

Somehow, I did figure out that it was OK to be sad. And even though they were sad, they had a party for my grandpa. My mother said it was for him, even though he wasn't there. I knew he would have liked the cake. But I wished he'd walk into the room and be there.

I wish my dog would walk up to us right now.

It's a big ache, isn't it? I understand how it feels because not very long after that, our dog died. He was old, too, like my grandpa. But when my dog died, no one came to the house for a party. When I was sad about my dog, people would just say, "Oh, you'll get another dog," or "You'll get over it in time," or "He was just a dog." Everybody acted as though nothing much had happened. It wasn't as OK to be sad or cry. And that just made me sadder. Nothing anybody said made me feel any better.

My aunt said some things like that. It kind of made me mad.

People often mean well. They just don't know what to say to cheer you up. There was one lady, though, who helped me make some sense of it all. That was Miss Elaine. She lived down the road from us, and she would come to the farm every week to buy eggs from my mother.

She came along one day shortly after my dog died. I was sitting on the porch steps feeling sad about my dog dying and about my grandpa dying and about how both my best buddies were gone. She sat on the steps with me for a bit, not saying a lot right away. She seemed to know my dog and my grandpa were on my mind.

Very quietly, she told me that when a good friend died, it helped her to think of life as a Big Play. All the people in the world—and animals like my dog—were the actors in the play. The actors all took turns going on stage, adding their bit to the play's story, then going behind the curtains, off stage, again. So my grandpa and my dog were nearby, just backstage. They weren't *gone* forever, just out of sight. And if I clapped my hands really hard and told them how much I loved how they played their parts in the Big Play, they would hear me clapping and they would feel my love through all the hurt.

I liked the idea of my dog and my grandpa being nearby, just behind a curtain where they could still hear me even if I couldn't see them. So I tried clapping my hands. It cheered me up a bit. Then Miss Elaine started clapping with me. Then we began clapping harder and harder and louder and louder! We made so much noise! Then we started laughing. My mother came out of the house to see what in the world was going on. When Miss Elaine went inside to get her eggs, I sat out on the porch feeling a little bit better than I did before.

Since then I've thought about the Big Play a lot, especially when something happens and I don't really understand why. It helps me think things through a little bit. It gives me a little bit of a different way of seeing things.

Could we clap for my dog?

Sure! Let's see who can clap louder!

IMAGINING

Thanks for clapping with me. That does make me feel a little better about my dog. He really was my special friend. And did you hear me whistle? I just learned to whistle and when I whistled my dog would come running SO fast!

I like thinking about my dog just being backstage where he can hear me clapping for him.

But who makes up the Big Play? Why couldn't they make it up so my dog didn't die?

Ah, well, as I imagine it, the Big Play is kind of messy compared to most plays.

Messy! Why?

Well, for one thing, most plays just have a few actors. But everyone in the whole world is in the Big Play together, all at the same time.

So EVERYBODY EVERYWHERE in the whole world is in the play at the same time?

That's how I imagine it.

Wow, that many people would need a really humongous stage!

We have one! The whole Earth is the stage for the Big Play.

So, dogs are actors, too? And all the other animals? And birds?

Yup. It isn't called the Big Play for nothing.

What about plants?

Well, a play needs some scenery, right?

So the grass and the trees and rain and the sky are all scenery, too, in the play?

Everything.   All the rocks and rivers and oceans and mountains and our houses and our cars—everything we can see is all part of the scenery in the Big Play.

Even my dog's toys?

Yup.

Who makes up the play?

Well, the way I imagine it, we all do. Together.

We do? What do you mean?

Well, nobody in particular makes up the whole script. We all kind of make it up together as we go along. We improvise.

What's a script? And what does improvise mean?

Well, in a usual play, someone writes a script. They write out exactly all the things all the actors are supposed to say and do. They describe where the actors should stand and how they should wave their arms and stomp around and all that.

The things the actors say are called their lines. The actors memorize their lines. That means they know them by heart and can say them without a script to read from. Then they practice saying their lines together. That's called a rehearsal. There's one person, a director, who tells them when to go out from behind the stage curtain onto the stage so the audience can see them. And the director tells them when to go backstage behind the curtain again.

The director tells the actors just how to say their lines the way the writer wants—like should they whisper their lines or should they shout them. Should they sound happy or sad or mad when they say them. And the director tells the actors where they should stand on the stage and whether they should wave or stomp or stand still or whatever else is written in the script.

Meanwhile, the director tells another bunch of people what kind of scenery to build. Different events in the play happen in different places. So they build scenery for each of those different places. Finally, the actors dress up in costumes that make them look like the characters they're playing in the play.

Everything about the play is decided before the actors go onstage. At last the actors are ready. They go onstage and speak their lines exactly the way the person who wrote them wrote them. They wave and stomp exactly the way the director directed them. During the play, different actors come and go, on and off the stage, when it's their turn. And at the end, ALL the actors come out together at the same time and bow to the audience. And the audience claps to let the actors know how much they liked the play and the way the actors acted it out.

The Big Play is lot messier. And much more fun, I think. For one thing, there are a lot more animals like dogs in it. For another, there's no script telling the actors exactly what to say. And there's no director telling the actors exactly how to move around on the stage. And it never actually begins in one place. And it just keeps going on and on. There's no ending.

In the Big Play, the actors think about what kind of part they want to play. Nobody tells them exactly what to say or what to do. They just go on the stage, see what's going on and jump right in. They may have some ideas about what they want to do in the play but they don't figure out exactly how they're going to wave or stomp or sing or dance until they get on stage. They all just make it up as they go along. That's improvising.

That's crazy! What if everybody tries to talk at the same time? Or run around at the same time? They'd be bumping into each other . . .

. . . and tripping over the dogs!

It sounds like a mess!

Messy, yes! Sometimes it is! But a lot more interesting than just following somebody's script. Think about your own day. You don't know exactly everything you're going to say or do when you get out of bed in the morning, do you?

Well, sort of. I know I'm going to go to school and stuff.

True enough. We all have routines, things we do pretty much the same way every day. And those are a bit like scripts. But what would happen if the school bus didn't come one morning because the driver got sick and they couldn't find a substitute in time?

I guess my mom or dad would have to take me to school.

There it is! That's you and your mom and dad improvising together.

And what if you got to school and because you were late, you hustled to get inside. And because you were hurrying, you tripped and fell. And when you fell, you cut your hand or your knee. Now what do you do?

I guess I'd go to the nurse's office to get the cut cleaned and get a bandage. Then I'd be REALLY late for class and I'd have to explain why to the teacher. And my teacher would probably ask someone in my class to help me catch up with whatever they were doing. Improvising, right?

Right. You and the nurse and the teacher and your classmates would all improvise together when a routine falls apart. Welcome to the Big Play!

The thing about having such a really Big Play with so many actors is that no one actor controls the whole thing. The story could go this way or that way depending on what each actor thinks or does or how whole bunches of actors act out at the time.

So I can't say why your dog died just now. Only that he did. Sometimes, down the road, we might come to understand that whatever happened happened for a reason. So something else could happen. Sometimes not. Maybe we'll figure it out when it's our turn to go back behind the stage curtain. I'd like to imagine that.

But when things that make me sad happen, I try to look for a different perspective, a different angle to see it from, a different way to look at the situation. That helps me feel a little better about it.

What do you mean?

Imagine, for instance, that when it was time for your dog to get ready to go on stage, your dog decided to be a certain kind of dog with a certain kind of personality. Say he wanted to be a friendly dog that loved to swim and eat ice cream. And then he picked out a costume that suited that personality, say a brown dog with webbed paddle paws for fast swimming.

And he might have decided that he would like to be a family dog so he had children to play with in a town that had places to swim. And maybe he even peeked from behind the curtain and saw your family on stage and thought, "Wow! I want to be *that* family's dog!" Then he got ready, waited for his cue to go on stage, and jumped out to join you.

You think my dog picked out our family? You think he picked me out to be his best friend?

I like to imagine that's possible.

So he loved me even before he became my dog?

I'd like to think that's possible, too.

Now I love my dog more than ever. And I'd still like to cuddle with him one more time. But I do feel a little better.

Can we clap for my dog again?

Sure. Ready? Set? Go!

CHAPTER 4

WHAT IF

Hi little neighbor! What's up at your house this afternoon?

My mom said to thank you for the pot of flowers you brought over yesterday. She said they cheered her up a little bit.

I'm glad. How about you? How are *you* feeling today?

Well, I liked the Big Play story you told me yesterday. It made me feel a little better about losing my dog. I told it to my mom. But I still miss my dog an awful lot. It was hard at school today to pretend everything was OK. My teacher told me to pay attention. And I'm really mad at my sister.

How come?

I think my sister left the gate open. She was the last one in the yard after we came home from soccer practice.

Did you see her leave it open?

No. But she was the last one in. How could she be so stupid? It was all her fault!

Hmmm. Could it have happened any other way?

Well, maybe. The mailman came by with a package for Mom. Maybe he left it open.

Sounds like that's a possibility, too.

And there was one time our dog got really excited when another dog was walking across the street. He scratched so hard at the gate that he jiggled the latch open. He was such a silly!

There you go. There's more than one possibility for why the gate was open.

So maybe it wasn't all my fault?

Ah, why do you say that?

Mom said I was supposed to be watching my little sister while we were outside in the yard.

I see. Well, it sounds to me like some improvising was going on.

Like the Big Play?

Exactly. So many actors, all moving around doing their own thing. You, your sister, your dog, the mailman, your mother, the lady who was driving the car. What if she had taken a different street? What if I had been walking by, saw the gate open and closed it? What if your dog had gone down the sidewalk instead of running into the street? No one can say exactly who completely caused what. All we know for sure is that there were a bunch of actors involved and when all the improvising came together, you lost your dog. That's what I meant about how the Big Play can get messy.

Yeah. I hadn't thought about what happened to my dog as improvising.

But I'm still mad. I'm mad at my mom. She took all my dog's stuff, his bed and his bowls and his toys and they're just gone. Just like my dog. And not seeing them anymore makes me miss my dog even more.

Maybe your mom misses your dog, too. Maybe she put his dishes and toys away for a while because seeing them made her sad. Did you ask her why she picked them up?

No. I'm mad at her. And I'm especially mad at my dad.

Seems like you're angry about a lot of things. Why are you mad at your dad?

He took our dog to the vet and never brought him home. I should have made sure the gate was closed. I loved my dog. I would never hurt him. But when my dad came home without our dog, I knew it was my fault. And I never got to see my dog again!

Well, remember that when the accident happened, your dad was improvising along with everyone else. What if he had brought your dog home? Would it have made you feel better to see your dog again, even if he wasn't breathing, wasn't moving? Or would that have made you feel even sadder?

I'm not sure. I only know I'm mad! It's not fair! Why couldn't the improvising go so that my dog was still here?

Well, imagine what might have happened if your dog hadn't run out of the yard.

Then he would still be here!

Maybe. But you told me that the gate was open and your little sister ran out on the sidewalk, too. So maybe your dog was a hero.

What?

Well, imagine he was playing in the yard and he saw the gate was open. He saw your little sister running toward the gate. He saw the car coming down the street. So he ran out in front of the car to try to stop it before it hit your sister. Maybe *he* saved *her.*

So you think my dog was a hero?

Maybe. I can imagine him doing that. I remember how he always barked at strangers and protected your family very bravely.

Yeah, he was like that. I never thought about my sister running into the street.

Or here's a crazy idea. Let's say your dog saw the car coming down the street. Maybe he decided he could show everyone how brave and fast he could be. He would race the car and chase it right off our street. Except that he forgot the part about how much bigger and faster cars are than dogs.

You mean my dog was improvising?

Maybe. It's hard to keep track of just what all the actors are up to all the time in the Big Play. Much less knowing why they're up to whatever it is they're doing. Maybe he just enjoyed the thrill of running as fast and as hard as he could and made a mistake. Maybe for some other reason we don't understand it was just his time to go backstage again. Can you imagine the story different ways?

I don't know. But I like making up stories about my dog. And it really makes me feel a little better to think my dog was a hero.

Me, too.

CHAPTER 5

KEEPING THE SPARKS ALIVE

Hi. What are you doing?

Well, I'm tending my dog garden.

Your dog garden! That sounds funny! Why do you call it a dog garden! Is it only for dogs?

I guess you could say that. See this little tree? It's a dogwood tree. And see those spotty leaves under the tree? Those are called dogtooth violets and they have pretty yellow flower bells every spring. That shrubby bush with little white flowers by the fence is called dog fennel. And these pretty flowers I'm planting right now are called dog flowers.

Those are just like the flowers you gave Mom yesterday. Why do they call them dog flowers?

Well, you take one of the blossoms and hold it just so, then squeeze it just so, and it looks like a tiny dog barking.

Can I try it?

Sure. Pick one.

Arf, arf! That's funny!

Most people around here call them snapdragons. Mrs. Chopra told me that in India where she grew up, the children called them dog flowers because you could make them look like they were barking. I liked that. So I decided to plant some in my dog garden.

A flower that barks! Can I take some home to show this to my sister?

Sure! Take as many as you like.

So you call it a dog garden because all the plants have dog names?

That, and also because two of our dogs are buried here.

You mean it's a dog cemetery?

Just for *our* dogs. One was very small. She was a feisty little terrier named Toby.

Toby! That's a boy's name.

Well, in her case, it was a girl's name. Our kids named her after a character in a book they liked. So that was that. Toby loved to snuggle on a particular blanket. So we wrapped her little body up nice and snuggly, tucked her into a really pretty box with her favorite toys, and now she's buried here. And we had a little celebration of her life. We clapped for her and told her what a great dog she'd been. The first dog that we put in the dog garden was a really BIG dog. It would have been hard to dig a hole deep enough for Roger.

Was Roger a boy?

Yes, he was a boy.

Then his name matched him.

Right. We found this dogwood when it was just a skinny little stick out in the woods on my brother's farm. We dug it up and put it in the ground here. Then we scattered Roger's ashes in there among its roots. We had a little celebration for him, too.

Roger's ashes? What do you mean?

Well, because Roger was so big, the veterinarian cremated him. That means they use really high heat to dry out the dog's body 'til it crumbles into a little pile of ashes. The ashes make it easier to bury the dog. Takes up less space. Some people keep the ashes someplace special in their house in a special box. Or they scatter them in a place that was special to the dog.

Does cremation hurt?

No, not at all. Remember how we talked about your dog's love spark? Once the spark flies off, the dog's body doesn't feel anything anymore. So it doesn't hurt.

I'm glad you stopped by to talk, by the way. I found something to show you. It's up on the porch. Come and I'll show you.

What is it?

It's my dog album. I've saved pictures in it of all the dogs I've known through the years.

Let me see! Are there pictures of Toby and Roger?

Yes there are. Let's sit down here first. My knees could use a break from gardening. Then I can lay this album on the table so we can open it up. Let's see . . . Toby and Roger are in this album somewhere. Here they are! Here and . . . here.

Wait. Turn those pages back again. What's this dog's name?

That's Sparky, the dog we had when I was very little, when I first learned about the Big Play.

Is that you in the picture?

Yes it is.

Sparky was cute. But I can't believe you were ever that little! What are these?

Those are letters to Toby. She died when my children were just a bit older than you are. They were sad, just like you, when they lost their dog. So we sat down and remembered all the things we loved about her, all the silly things she liked to do, her favorite things to eat, and things like that. We wrote letters to her, kind of like writing down the story of her life. Then we put them here in the album.

I like the pictures they drew of her on their letters. All her spots. And that ball looks just like the tennis balls my dog loved to chase and chew up.

She did love to chase balls, just like your dog. And then she'd bury them. She was always digging. Especially in the dog garden!

You make me laugh.

Well, that's a good sign.

A sign of what?

A sign that you're feeling a little better. And a sign that maybe you're ready to think about playing with your dog again.

Playing with my dog again? How?

Remember when I told you that you can't understand the Big Play unless you can imagine things? Well, you can imagine that you and your dog are still buddies. That's why I like this album. I can look at it and remember the fun times I had with my dogs. And sometimes I close my eyes and go play with them again.

Close your eyes and go play?

Closing my eyes sometimes helps me imagine. Would you like me to show you how I bring my dogs back into my life again for a little while?

That sounds neat. Is it hard?

Not at all. Remember when you first moved next door and you wanted a dog so badly? You talked and talked to me about getting a dog. You told me what color fur it would have and how big it would be and what kind of ears it would have. You had quite the shopping list! Seeing your dog again only takes a bit of that same imagination you used to bring your dog into your life in the first place.

So you just close your eyes? Like you're going to sleep?

Well, I guess I do get quiet, and maybe a bit dreamy. But I don't go to sleep like a nap.

Can we go see my dog?

Sure we can. First thing is to get comfy right here in our chairs, and relax and just chill a little bit with our eyes closed.

Then we'll take a few nice, slow breaths in and out, in and out, slowly in and out.

Keep your eyes closed but look up, ever so softly, behind your eyelids. Gently, don't force it. Just pretend you're look-ing up into the leaves of the little dogwood tree over there.

Feel yourself get very quiet, quiet enough to hear those whispers from behind the stage curtains.

And the soft feeling behind our eyes kind of moves down and settles in our hearts. And our hearts open up like the petals of beautiful flowers. And behind our eyelids, in our mind's eye, we imagine that we're sitting in your house.

Now from our hearts, we softly call your dog.

You hear a scratch at the door and you go to investigate.

You open the door.

Your dog is standing there, right in front of you. His tail is wagging and wagging. He's panting and whining. He's so excited to see you.

And you're so excited to see him. You pet him and pet him, and hug him and hug him. You look at his big brown eyes and he wags his tail.

You realize that he wants you to take him for a walk and you're so ready to go with him. The two of you go outside, out the gate and down the street to the park.

Your dog has brought a toy! He runs ahead of you, teasing you with the toy. You run after him, so happy to be playing with him again.

You play and play so hard that you both flop down on the ground. Your dog licks your face. You pet his head and rub his ears. You are so glad to see each other again.

When you catch your breath, you realize it's time to go home.

You and your dog walk home, so happy to be together.

You get to the gate and open it. But your dog sits on the sidewalk, staying outside. His tail wags with the promise to come back to play again whenever you call him.

You stroke his soft head. You promise to call him back to play again soon. He picks up his toy and walks away.

You turn and come back into the house. You sit for a moment enjoying the warm feeling of the love you and your dog share.

Now slowly open your eyes. And take deep breath. And another.

What did you see?

Wow! It was awesome to imagine being with my dog again. I thought it would make me sad but it didn't. I really could feel my dog's love! Do you think he felt mine?

Oh, yes.

That's kind of like imagining a play, isn't it? We just made up a play about me and my dog, didn't we?

Yes, we did. You can use your imagination to play with your dog again, wherever you want, whenever you want. Just talk to your dog. Just play with your dog. Tell your dog anything. Tell your dog how you feel because you can't still feel and smell and hug him. Then go ahead and imagine you're doing those things anyway.

Even though your dog's furry self isn't with you, his love spark *is*. You can connect with your dog whatever way feels good to you. You can hold a picture of your dog or a stuffed dog that reminds you of your dog if you want.

Do you think my dog saw the play we imagined?

More than that. His love spark was right there on stage with you, improvising and loving every minute of it. And right now I can imagine he'd like to connect with some of the cake I made this afternoon. Let me go get some— and some lemonade?—while you look at that album some more.

CHAPTER 6

POSSIBILITIES

Welcome home, little neighbor. I was just finishing up my gardening when I saw your bus pull up. Lots of homework tonight? That backpack is bulging with books! And it looks like my mailbox is bulging with catalogs! Is that a new friend I saw you waving at when you got off the bus?

Yeah, I have a lot to read. And that girl just moved here and she's in my class this year. We both like our teacher. And we both like dogs!

I told her about my dog. And she said that when dogs die, they go over a Rainbow Bridge to a big, like, playground. They get to stay there and play there with lots of other dogs and other animals. Then when we die, we get to cross the Rainbow Bridge. And when we get to the other side, our dogs come running to greet us. We get to be together again. Is that true?

Who knows for sure? I've heard of the Rainbow Bridge, though. I can certainly imagine what it looks like. It certainly feels good to imagine that we'll see our pets again. But if my animal friends all come running at once, I'm in trouble!

Why?

Well, in my life, I've been with a whole lot of dogs and other animals like cows and horses and chickens. If they all meet me at the Rainbow Bridge at the same time, they'll knock me over with their running and jumping and flapping and licking and prancing!

That would be messy! Like the Big Play, huh! Is the Rainbow Bridge like heaven?

Who knows? There are so many ideas about heaven! That's another one of those words that upsets some grown-ups. If your idea about heaven is different than what they think about it, then they want to argue with you. Some people don't think there's a heaven place at all. Then there are other people who believe they died, went to heaven and then came back again! But each of them tells a different story about what it was like there. So...heaven knows exactly what heaven is like!

What happens when dogs go backstage in the Big Play? Is that like heaven?

Well, I suppose you could think of it that way, that when an actor goes off stage behind the curtains and you can't see them anymore, they've gone to heaven. What do you imagine that would be like?

I think I'd like to imagine my dog would come back out on the stage and be with me again.

Well, let's imagine that your dog was backstage for a long long long time. Ten years! Maybe more. Then, one day, you were walking along minding your own business and suddenly there he was! Standing right in front of you again! What would you do?

I'd be so happy!

Or you'd be so freaked out, you'd scream. Aaah! A ghost! Oh no! What do I do!

No I wouldn't. Well, maybe. I'd be pretty surprised. Maybe I wouldn't believe it.

Right. But here's something different to imagine. What if your dog went backstage for a while, then decided to go back onstage as a different character wearing a different costume? And what if your dog's love spark was actually not just a spark but a ball of sparks. And the ball burst and scattered little sparks all over. And each little spark grabbed a different costume and bounced out onto the stage.

Now imagine you come across a whole litter of bouncy squirmy puppies. And you look at them and one gives you a particular feeling, a feeling like the feeling you had with your old dog. And the puppy acts just a little bit like your old dog used to act. And you'd say to yourself, I feel like I know that dog.

Could that happen?

Well, things in nature do seem to happen in cycles that go around and around. The sun comes up once a day and goes down once a day. Every day. The tides down by the beach come up and go down twice a day. Individual things themselves change a bit this way or that but the general cycle of things keeps on going the same way, over and over.

Take the flowers here in my dog garden. Especially that dog fennel! When it goes to sleep in the winter, I cut the dead stalks back to the ground. In spring, it sends up new green shoots. All summer, it's covered with pretty little flowers. Come fall, the flowers produce seeds and they scatter all over the garden. And every year, the dog fennel and I go through the same cycle. And every spring, it grows back a little bit the same but a little bit different.

So I can imagine that as things come and go, and go around and around, some day you might find a dog that reminds you a lot of your old dog, even if that dog isn't exactly like your old dog.

Can I tell you something weird? When I climbed into bed last night, I thought I heard my dog's collar tags jingling. I told my sister and she said I was crazy. She said I was just making it up. And my mom said it was just my imagination. But I'm SURE I heard them.

Well, you know I believe in imagination. I see the Rainbow Bridge and the Big Play and our memories of our pets as imaginary bridges that keep us connected to them. They help us keep them in our hearts and in our minds. And bridges work both ways.

What do you mean?

Well, have you ever been in a school play when someone forgets where they're supposed to be standing. Or—even worse—forgets what they're supposed to say? And then from behind the curtain, the teacher helps them out? She whispers the lines they're supposed to say just loud enough for them to hear her but not loud enough for anybody in the audience to hear.

I've heard a lot of people say they thought they heard their dog or smelled their dog. Or they even say they saw their dog out of the corner of their eye. Just a quick flash of fur. Just like you heard tags jingling. I like to imagine those are little stage whispers from dogs, letting their people know they're still nearby. Just behind the curtains. Reminding their people that they still love them. So you can tell your sister that I don't think you're crazy.

Speaking about gardens and cycles, would you like a little dogwood tree to remind you of your dog? I have some potted up in the backyard. Grew them from seeds from that dogwood tree here in my front yard. They're ready to put in the ground now. You can have one if you'd like. Ask your mom. Come back and get it if she says yes.

That would be awesome! I'll go ask her right now!

CHAPTER 7

PLANTING SEEDS

Thanks for the dogwood tree. And guess what? Guess! You're never going to guess what we did with it!

I can't imagine! You're so excited, it must be something really amazing. Tell me.

Well, I told my mom about the dog album. And the Rainbow Bridge and the Big Play. And clapping and everything. And I told her how sad I was that I didn't get to say good-bye to my dog and how all his stuff went away. And GUESS WHAT?

I'm going to pop if you don't tell me!

Mom didn't throw away all my dog's stuff! She just put it away for a while because, just like you said, it made her so sad to see the toys and bowls and leashes around the house. And THEN my dad came home with a box from the vet. He said it had my dog's ashes in it. So they didn't just leave my dog at the vet and throw him away. I was so glad!

And THEN you know what happened?!

I'm listening.

We had a party for my dog! My sister and I drew pictures. I drew a picture of my dog. My sister drew a whole page full of bones for him. He loved bones. And we had cookies. And ice cream. And we decided to make a dog garden for him!

My mom put my dog's leash and a couple of his old toys into a pretty cardboard box. Dad dug a big, deep hole in the corner of the yard, next to the fence. We poured my dog's ashes into the bottom. Then we put the box in. Then we put the dogwood tree on top of that.

My sister helped me shove all the dirt back in the hole. Dad pushed the dirt down with his foot and pounded a big stake in next to the tree. Then he tied the tree to the stake so it would stay straight. Mom said it looks tall and proud.

Mom planted the dog flowers you gave us and then she dumped a bag of mulch around, just like in your garden. So we have a dog garden now, too! I like the idea of my dog being in our yard again.

And I imagine he likes being there, too. Did you hear your dog's tags jingling again?

What? Do you think my dog was there?

Well, I can imagine him just behind the stage curtains, peeking out, and watching how everyone in your family was showing how much they loved him. I'm sure it made him feel really, really happy. Because it shows you haven't forgotten him. You still have a love connection. And he can stay alive in your imaginations forever.

We clapped for him! Maybe he heard us. But he's not really alive anymore, is he?

Well, not in the sense that you need to feed him and give him water and take him for walks anymore. But I imagine that his little love spark is very much alive in your life. And you can bring it back any time you remember him in your heart. In your imagination, you can still hug him and play with him.

Like we did the other day?

Right. Like that.

Could we do that again?

Certainly. Last time we imagined your dog was playing with you at the park. Where would you like to meet him today?

In his dog garden! In my yard, where we planted the tree for him. Just in case he wasn't watching. I want to tell him all about it. And how even though I'm not as sad as I was before, I still miss him. And I won't forget him. Ever.

OK. Let's sit up on the porch again. Get yourself settled and we'll send your dog some imaginary pictures of all the things your family did for him. Do you remember how we started before?

Yes! Sit still, close your eyes, do some breaths and look up a little inside your eyelids. But keep your eyes closed.

That's wonderful! You're a good listener and you have a good memory!

So just like you remembered, we'll sit still and get comfy.

Now we'll close our eyes and take a few nice breaths. In and out, in and out, in and out. Hmmmmm. Now our eyes look up, ever so softly and gently, behind our eyelids.

And we can see behind our eyelids, in our mind's eye, that we're in your yard. We're sitting right in front of the little dogwood tree in your new dog garden.

And the soft feeling moves down and settles around our hearts. And our hearts open up like beautiful dogwood flowers in spring. Now from our hearts, we softly call your dog.

We ask your dog to join us in your yard to see his new garden.

Can you see your dog coming from behind the curtain? He's so happy that you haven't forgotten him. He's so glad that you called him to play again.

You show him the new dog garden. That's for you, you tell him.

We planted a dogwood tree so we'll never forget you.

Tell your dog all about the things you planted with the dogwood tree to remember him. Show him some mind pictures of you planting them in the dog garden.

Tell him how you'll remember him every time you see the little tree. Tell him that he can come back and play in the yard and see the tree again whenever he wants.

Play with your dog a while.

Then call your dog and give him a hug. Remind him that you'll never forget him. Tell him you love him.

Now let him go backstage again.

Say thank you. Say good-bye, until the next time. And enjoy the warm feeling in your heart as long as you like.

Then open your eyes whenever you want.

Thanks. That makes me feel better about my dog. I still miss him but he doesn't feel as "gone" as he did before. I think he liked it, too.

I certainly imagine that he did.

CHAPTER 8

SAY WHAT?

Hi. What are you doing in your dog garden?

I'm looking for a glove I lost. I was using my gardening gloves yesterday and now one of them is missing. I have a hunch it's somewhere over here. Want to help?

Sure. But what's a hunch?

It's a kind of suggestion or feeling, an idea that just seems to come out of nowhere about something that's on your mind. Sometimes it's like being nagged. The same notion keeps popping into your head over and over again. And I have a nagging feeling that my glove is somewhere over here, even though I don't remember working over here yesterday.

How do you get a hunch?

Oh, mostly they just seem to come to people. Just pops into your head. But sometimes I ask Toby to help me find things. Then when an idea, a hunch, pops into my head, I pay attention to it.

You mean your dog Toby, the one you told me about? Isn't she buried here in the dog garden?

Yes, she is. That's the rock we used to mark where we buried her.

How can you ask her to help you find things?

Oh, it's a game we played when she was alive. So I imagine I'm playing it with her again and it keeps me from getting all upset about whatever I lost until I find it again.

Toby's favorite favorite favorite game was finding things. She had such a good nose. She was always sniffing and exploring. And digging, too! We would show her something like a shoe or a toy or a cookie. Then we'd hide it and tell her to go find it. I can't remember hiding anything that she didn't eventually find. Even when we hid it inside something, and then hid THAT inside something else, she always found it. She had an amazing nose!

Even though she's gone, I like to imagine that Toby's little love spark is still as busy as ever and we can still play the find it game. I tell her what I've lost and put her to work on it. I just go about my business until I get a hunch. Then I follow the hunch. I usually find whatever I've lost when I ask her to help.

So when I lost my glove, I just asked Toby to help me find it. Then I stopped worrying about it and went about my business. I just waited for a hunch. And my hunch was to look around here, even though I wasn't working here yesterday.

Does it work?

As long as I imagine it will work, it seems to happen.

So you think up a play in your mind, like we did yesterday?

Actually, it's even simpler than that. I just think of Toby and call her name, just like I did when she was still here. And I trust her little spark will come running to find me. Then I talk to her, tell her my problem. And ask her to show me where to find whatever I can't find. Then I just wait until I get a hunch about it.

Pretty much I talk to her the same way I did when she was here with me. We didn't stop being pals just because she died.

I haven't told anyone at school about how we imagine playing with my dog. They would think I'm crazy.

You think so? To me, talking to Toby is just another way of letting my mind play with possibilities. Just a different way than what we did to imagine playing with your dog yesterday. Maybe I've just imagined I can still talk to Toby's little spark so many times over the years that it just seems natural to me now.

Look! Over here! Behind the dogwood tree, up against the fence!

My glove! Thank you! Now I remember. I was carrying the gloves and set them down on top of the fence when I went out to get the garbage can. I must have picked one up and knocked the other off into the dog garden without noticing. And thank you, Toby!

Why are you thanking her when she's dead?

Oh, it's always important to say thank you when you get help. Gratitude feeds and waters the love sparks all around us and makes them keep growing. Very, very important, saying thank you.

Could I ask my dog to help me with things?

Certainly. Why not? Just call him and ask away.

Do you think he could help me find my homework?

Hmmm. That might be a little different. Is it really lost?

Sort of.

Right. So maybe you need to *do* your homework first before you ask your dog to help find the homework that's not even started so it can't actually be lost yet? Getting help doesn't work THAT way! But I think you already know that, little neighbor.

How did you know I haven't done it yet?

Well, since you just got off the bus and your books are still in your backpack, I figured maybe your homework assignment was in there. But the homework wasn't actually done yet.

Was that a hunch?

No, just good guessing.

Are you always a good guesser?

Sometimes. Not always! What is your homework today?

I have some math. That's easy for me. Then I'm supposed to write a story about flowers and draw a picture to go with it. I can't think of what to write. It's such a lame assignment.

What about asking your dog to help you with it?

Really?

Why not? You could beat your brains out trying to think up a topic. Or you could just wait for a hunch, like I did with my glove. Or another option is to try closing your eyes and asking your dog to help you see what to write about.

I know! I've got it!

Wow! That was fast.

Yeah! As soon as I just closed my eyes, I saw our dog garden. I'll draw that! And tell about the dog flowers and their little jaws!

Sounds like a winner, little neighbor. Head home and get to work. Can't wait to see your picture story!

First I'll get a snack. Then I'll write about the dog garden! See you tomorrow.

CHAPTER 9

LOVE CYCLES

Why the long face?

A girl on the bus said that the Rainbow Bridge was stupid and the Big Play was stupid and I'm never going to see my dog again. Ever. His spark burned out. She was mean. I told her she was ugly. U-G-L-Y. Ugly.

She did say some mean, hurtful things. And her kind of thinking steered the Big Play in a messy, not-so-good-feeling direction and here you are feeling bad. And that made you angry, made you want to make her feel bad, too. So you called her ugly.

Yeah!

Did that make you feel any better?

I don't know about feeling better. But I got back at her!

Could we find a thought that might help steer you back toward feeling better?

What do you mean? How?

Well, thinking mean thoughts steers the Big Play in a mean direction. Thinking kind thoughts steers it in a kind direction. We can choose how we want to improvise. We can't change what other people choose to think and say, but we can choose what we think and say.

I don't want to be nice to her.

Well, that's a choice. How does that make you feel?

Mean, like her, I guess.

Remember when we imagined different reasons why your dog might have run out in the street? And it made you feel a little better to think of him as a hero? Could you feel a little kinder toward the girl if you knew she was going home with a bad grade on a paper? And she knew her mom was going to be really mad? Or what if she just lost *her* dog and no one was helping her deal with feeling sad? So she took her feelings out on you.

I guess that would make me feel a little bit sorry for her. Maybe I would have just made a face at her instead of feeling mean and calling her ugly.

So imagine something like that, something that helps you feel a little kinder, and put that thought into the Big Play.

I didn't really believe her about my dog. I was just mad because she said it in front of all the other kids and tried to make me look stupid. I just wanted to get back at her.

I know.

Remember when I told you about the celebration we had for my dog? Well, there was something else we did, after we planted the dog garden.

From the look on your face, it was something serious.

It was. Kind of. We talked about getting another dog.

And you aren't sure about that?

I still keep wishing my old dog could come back. I still miss him. And if he's backstage in the Big Play, I don't want him to think I don't care about him anymore. I still love him. It would be fun to have a dog to play with again. But I don't want my old dog to be sad. Maybe he misses me as much as I miss him. I don't want him to think I'm forgetting him.

Is that true? Would you forget about your old dog if you had a new dog?

Well, I guess not really. But, like, my dog was just always there for me. Always. No matter what I did. Or even when I wasn't so nice to him. At the playground, he always stayed with me. He never ran off with any other kids. He was so . . . .

Loyal?

Yeah. Like that. I could always count on him, trust him. I feel like I'd be letting him down to get another dog. That makes me feel bad to think about getting another dog. But then I think it would be fun to have a dog again. And that makes me feel good. I just don't know.

It's OK not to know what to do. Or to be unsure if what you're feeling is good or bad. Confusing, but perfectly normal. Everyone bounces around like that after they lose someone they love.

They do?

Sure. You know, love relationships like the one between you and your dog run in cycles, too. They're just like the cycles we talked about before. They're like plants coming up in spring, blooming into flowers, then going to seed, and tucking themselves back into the ground again for the winter. Comings and goings. Comings and goings. One ends. Another begins. What seems to be an ending becomes a beginning.

Our job is just to keep going and learn what we can about life from the way our pet lived and died. To learn how to treat other people a little differently because of the way our pet treated us.

What do you mean keep going?

Well, it's normal to feel bad when you lose a pet. And it takes some time to deal with those mixed up feelings. But if you keep on recycling your sad feelings over and over, you can get stuck there. You need to figure out a way to get unstuck and get going again with things that make you not sad, things you like to do that make you feel good.

Like when we can't get the WiFi connection for our games and my mom unplugs the box then plugs it back in to start it again?

Something like that. Good example.

But how do people do that? Sometimes I feel better about losing my dog, but then I feel sad again.

Well, it can be very simple. But for a lot of people, it's hard.

Why?

Oh, lots of reasons. Sometimes feeling bad gets attention from other people. And if you like that attention, you might not want to stop those feelings.

Yeah. I get that. Since my dog died, my mom's been letting us have a lot more cookies and ice cream instead of giving us peanut butter sandwiches and carrots after school!

I like cookies and ice cream, too. Wouldn't want that to stop!

And I can see how thinking about getting another dog might make you feel a little better. But then you feel guilty about wanting another dog and that makes you feel bad again.

Yeah, that's how I feel right now.

And so it goes. You bounce back and forth. We have the choice to cry or clap. But if you decide to reach for a little bit of a good feeling whenever a bad feeling drags you down, you eventually get yourself unstuck. You bounce one way, then the other, and back again. And as you keep working little by little to get unstuck, your heart starts to make a little room, and then a little more room, and soon there can be enough room for a new dog to wiggle in.

I could never love another dog as much.

Maybe. Maybe you'll never love another dog just the same way. But maybe you'll find you can love one just as much. Or even more. Letting go of the hurt doesn't mean you don't care about your dog. And it doesn't mean you don't love your dog anymore. Or that your dog won't keep on loving you.

Remember, we're all in the Big Play. And we can choose our lines. Can you imagine the play a little bit? Instead of thinking, "What if my dog was still here," could you think, "What if I had a dog again like my old dog"?

Tell me, was your old dog always perfect? Always good?

Well, no. Sometimes he took food off the kitchen counter when we weren't home. And he barked like crazy and knocked things over running to the door whenever the package man came. And . . .

And?

. . . if I left my sneakers out of the closet, he chewed the laces up. That made Mom really really mad! At my dog and at me! And if I didn't pay attention, he'd try to eat my ice cream when

we went for cones. When he did that stuff, Mom used to say, "You little badness!"

Well, would you want another dog that did ALL those things all over again?

Maybe. But probably not.

So now you have a chance to imagine a dog that has all the things you liked about your old dog but not any of his "badness."

What do you mean?

Well, as you think about the kind of new dog that might be fun to have, you might say things like "My new dog loves to fetch balls," "My new dog loves to sit and read with me," "My new dog loves to swim as much as I do," and "I would like to have a dog with floppy ears." Pretty soon you'd have a good list of things that would be nice to have in a new dog.

Kind of like a dog recipe!

Exactly! And that's another way the things you think about steer the direction of the Big Play.

Think about backstage in the Big Play. The stagehands are listening. They hear your list of dog ingredients. They look around at all the dogs waiting to go onstage and find one that has every single ingredient. And they get the dog's costume ready, and at just the right time, out he goes on stage and runs up to greet you.

So I can imagine the most amazing, best-ever dog in the world?

Whatever you want. But be prepared for surprises!

What do you mean?

Well, for one thing, maybe the stagehands will put the ingredients together in a way you hadn't thought about. You asked for floppy ears but you forgot to mention legs. So your new dog has lovely long floppy ears but he has short legs. So his long floppy ears drag on the ground and they're always wet and muddy when he runs to give you a doggy kiss.

Or maybe you ask for a dog that loves to chase balls and get one that's the best chaser and catcher ever. But he just runs away with the balls. He doesn't want to bring them back for you to throw again. And maybe your sister was thinking about a dog with certain ingredients and your mom was thinking about a dog with certain ingredients, too. When the stagehands find a dog with ALL of those ingredients, your mom and your sister and you might ALL be surprised! Be careful what you wish for, they say. Remember, we're all improvising together.

Hmmm, can I suggest an ingredient, too? How about a quiet dog that doesn't bark and wake up my dog too early in the morning!

Sure! But what will happen to my old dog if we get a new dog? Will his spark go out? Maybe the girl on the bus was right. Maybe he'd be gone forever.

No, your dog's spark is love and love never dies. Love is what the Big Play is all about. Your dog loved you, even when you scolded him. Or when you did something the grown-ups might have thought of as "badness," your dog still loved you. And you loved your dog even when he chewed up a shoe or snatched your ice cream or some other kind of doggy "badness." You learned about love from each other.

Can you still imagine your dog standing backstage behind the curtain in the Big Play? Can you imagine him out of sight but still wiggling and wagging when he sees you, still loving you and encouraging you to be the best you can as you play your part in the play? Every time you remember your dog, you keep that love spark alive. And your dog sends love right back to you. Love keeps us connected.

He really was a great dog. I still miss him. But I guess I could talk to my mom and dad and sister about dog ingredients. That might be fun to think about.

There's something else that might be fun to think about. All that talk about ice cream made me want some. Run home and ask your mom if I can treat you and your sister to after-school cones at Toto's.

Can we buy a cone for my dog, too?

Absolutely. What flavor do you imagine he would like?

He can have anything but chocolate. Chocolate isn't good for dogs. But we're being silly, aren't we? How would he eat the cone?

Oh, I imagine the three of us can find a way to make an extra cone disappear without a problem.

EPILOGUE

Sammy! Sammy! Hushhhh. Hushhhh. I know you love seeing Doogie but you don't need to broadcast it to the whole neighborhood!

You'd better hang on to that leash before Doogie jumps over the fence into my yard to join his girlfriend here!

You say such funny things! Do you really think Doogie and Sammy are boyfriend-girlfriend?

Well, maybe not exactly in the way you might have a crush on someone at school. But dogs do like the company of other dogs and these two seem to have hit it off pretty well ever since you and your sister started walking him for Mrs. Gordon. How about I get Sammy's leash and we take them for a walk together?

Sure! And, anyway, speaking of Doogie . . . there's something I wanted to talk to you about.

Oh? Give me a minute to close up the house up and grab the leash.

OK. We're ready to go. So what's on your mind?

Mrs. Gordon is going to sell her house.

I heard that. When I visited her in the hospital, she still wasn't able to talk very well, or move one arm, or even get out of bed. She's doing better now that she's home but I wondered if she could stay there, even with help.

Her son Jack asked my sister and me to walk Doogie once a day for her. He wanted to pay us but Mom wouldn't let him at first. She said it was just the neighborly thing to do, to help them with Doogie. But after a couple of weeks, he insisted and she gave in. Know what we did?

Tell me.

We started a puppy fund to get a new dog. We put all the walking money in it.

What did your mom and dad say about that?

Dad's been all for getting another dog. But Mom says she isn't quite ready to deal with a new puppy. She's says it's a lot of work and a lot of time to housebreak a puppy. And it wouldn't be fair to leave a puppy for a long time on the days she's at work.

Puppy training can take time, for sure. I thought we'd never get our little Toby terrier housebroken. But, by and by, she figured out that potty business was an outside job, not an inside one.

But, guess what?

No idea! Tell me.

Yesterday, Jack asked us if we would like to have Doogie for our own dog.

Really!

He stops to see Mrs. Gordon every day on his way home from work. Yesterday, when I went to walk Doogie, he said that the doctor doesn't think she'll be able to stay at home alone anymore.

She said something along those lines when I visited her Monday. So how do you feel about Jack's offer? If she can't stay at the house, I know she'll be worried about what will happen to Doogie.

Well, Mrs. Gordon is thinking she might move into that retirement place over on Grant Street. It's closer to Jack's house when she wants to go there. And Jack said they have a big garden and kitchen for the people who live there to use if they want. So she can still do some of the things she likes.

Anyway, Jack said we could have Doogie on one condition.

What's that?

If she moves there, he wants us to walk Doogie over to visit her once a week.

How do you kids feel about that?

Well, it's not very far to walk from here. Mom and Dad said it's up to my sister and me.

Sounds like you're not entirely sure about it, though.

Maybe. It's not about the walking him over for visits. And we really like Doogie. He's a neat dog. It's just that my sister and I have been thinking about puppies. We've talked about what kind of dogs we like. I like labs but Mom and Dad think we should get a little smaller dog. My sister likes Yorkies but Dad thinks they might not be up to all the hiking stuff we like to do. Then when Jack said we could have Doogie and we talked about taking him, Mom got out the dog recipe. Remember when I told you we made one?

I remember when you said that, but you never told me exactly what ingredients you put in it.

That's the thing. Doogie has just about all the ingredients we put in the recipe. Except he's not a puppy and we don't know if he can swim. We want a dog that can swim with us like our old dog.

That's interesting.

Yeah. But THAT's the thing! Mom noticed that we never wrote "puppy" as an ingredient, even though that's what my sister and I were thinking. We just wrote down "Things We Want in a Dog" at the top of the list. We never actually said "puppy," just "dog."

Well that IS interesting!

We really do like Doogie but it would also be fun to have a puppy to play with. We told Jack and Mrs. Gordon we'd let them know this weekend.

What will happen to Doogie if you don't take him?

Jack said he'd try to find another family to take him. His son is allergic to dogs and gets hives and all sneezy around Doogie even he takes some kind of allergy pill first. So they aren't sure it would work if they take him. But Mrs. Gordon wants Doogie to have a really nice home, a special home, he said, where she would know that Doogie felt loved like she loves him.

So, on the one hand, a puppy means a lot of time and work to housebreak and train and, on the other hand, there's Doogie, already house trained. But a puppy would be more playful and fun than a grown dog like Doogie?

Not exactly. Doogie likes to play, too. He's great at fetching! That's how Mrs. Gordon exercised him. But I kind of thought it would be fun to train a dog myself, to teach it tricks.

Does Doogie already knows everything a dog can learn? Can he jump through your sister's hula-hoop? Can he find things you hide? Can he roll over? If he doesn't know how to swim, could *you* teach him?

He does some things. Like sit and stay and fetch. But not every-thing. Not those other things you said. I guess I could teach him new things, huh? Like he was a puppy? He's pretty smart. He already knows all of our walking routes and when we're head-ing home, he goes out in front and leads the way. It's as if he's walking me!

In my experience, the fun of teaching a dog new things can go on as long as you have the interest and patience to do it. Doogie is still a young dog. And he sure seems to like you kids.

Yeah, he does. Mom said we're going to talk again about taking him or not at dinner tonight. We can vote about it and everyone's vote counts.

How do you think that might go?

Well, Mom and Dad will probably vote for taking him. I'm not sure about my sister. And after talking about it, I think I'll vote . . . .

Doogie! Leave Sammy alone! They're so funny together. It looks like he's trying to kiss her.

The way they behave, I have to agree. If you gave her a say in whether or not Doogie moves in next door, I think Sammy would bark a loud "yes." Let's head back to my house and see if we can find any cookies.

Dog cookies or people cookies? Doogie and I BOTH love cookies!

I have a hunch we can find something for all our neighbors when we get back home. What do you think, Sammy?

The End

ACKNOWLEDGMENTS

No one ever writes a book alone. Looking back over this book's gestation, I count so many people whose encouragement and support moved it along. How remarkable it is that a single kind word, spoken at the right time, can make such a difference in an outcome. I owe thanks to many more than are mentioned here.

Family first. Always. My husband Bob gave me the means and the space to make some major life shifts so that this book could happen. I love him for knowing when to cheerlead and when to critique while I searched for the middle way. As a group, our sons Charlie and Paul and their wives Allison and Erin provided a supportive sounding board. My sisters Carol O'Shea and Sue Squiller listened and encouraged. My cousin Bette Haney's suggested readings pointed in new directions.

As the book took form, comments from early readers improved it greatly. I appreciate the time and willingness to help offered by Gail Bernson, Carolyn Cary, Jeanette Ciciora, Lyn Conway, Phyllis Das, Debbie Devenny, Raffaello Di Meglio, Linnea Ehri, Victoria Hadden, Lisa Jacoby, Paul Kreitler and Erin Sherer Kreitler, Antoinette Martignoni, Rev.

Dr. Richard McCaughey, Carol O'Shea, Debbie Rick Selski, Dr. Kathleen Smiler, Vivian Sorvall, and Sue Squiller. Robin Quinn shaped the book's final form through her thoughtful developmental suggestions, editing, and proofing. Tricia Breidenthal's graphic talents frosted the cake inside and out.

Carole Ohl's magical zentangle-style illustrations complement the story's invitation to imagine. The illustrations portray dogs that once played among us. I would like to thank Harper and Dan Braine, Phyllis and Pranab Das, Erin Sherer Kreitler and Paul Kreitler, Ariane Mermod, Dr. Kathleen Smiler, Vivian Sorval, and Sue Squiller for sharing their dog photos and stories (read them all online at ramblingdogpublications.com).

My meditation group's support kept me going as I struggled with new ways of understanding life's events and writing in a new genre. The group's members shifted from time to time but you know who you are. My thanks for always offering the kind of nonjudgmental comradery we usually enjoy only from our pets.

Grateful thanks to gentle Remy, the dog who was always close by as the book moved from a vague concept to manuscript. Curled up near my computer, she kept me company through every keystroke but went behind the curtain just before the words made their final transition into book form. Her timing called me to walk my talk.

My deepest gratitude to Raffaello Di Meglio and to Dick and Meredith McCaughey who, by providing perspectives that made grief a bit more bearable when our first grandchild died full term in utero, planted the seeds from which this book grew.

Bonnie Kreitler

ABOUT
THE AUTHOR

Family lore holds that **Bonnie Kreitler**'s deep connection to animals began even before she started talking. When she learned to read and write, she began hand printing illustrated stories and has rarely been without pencil, pen or keyboard nearby since. She worked as a journalist and marketing consultant in the horse industry for over 25 years. Her book *50 Careers with Horses* was a best seller in its niche. Learning to meditate led to studies of intuitive techniques and energy healing including animal communication and Reiki. She counts herself fortunate to enjoy a career that combines her love of animals with her writing skills. *I Heard Your Dog Died* is her first fiction work. Bonnie lives in Fairfield, Connecticut. Learn more at rambling dogpublications.com.

Photo credit: Carole Ohl

ABOUT THE ILLUSTRATOR

Graphic designer **Carole Ohl** lives in Dayton, Ohio, where she runs Bead Stash, a bead store. She became a certified Zentangle® teacher in 2010 after a beading friend bugged her to check out the drawing technique online. She authors the *Tangle-A-Day Calendar* published by Braughler Books. See more of her tangling at openseedarts.blogspot.com.

ABOUT THE ZENTANGLE-STYLE ART IN I HEARD YOUR DOG DIED

The Zentangle art form and method was created by Rick Roberts and Maria Thomas. Zentangle® is a registered trademark of Zentangle, Inc. Learn more at zentangle.com.

The dogs illustrated in this book were real dogs who touched their owner's lives in remarkable ways. Read their stories and learn how to create a zentangle-style drawing of your own dog at ramblingdogpublications.com

DISCLAIMER
& RESOURCES

This book is fiction. Any resemblance to persons living or dead is purely coincidental.

The author wishes that anyone feeling bad after losing a pet will feel a little better after reading it. The author makes no claim to counseling credentials and does not intend the book as a substitute for professional support. Any actions taken or not taken because of reading this book are the sole responsibility of the reader.

If a reader is struggling to reconcile their feelings after a loss or unable to cope with their grief, the author urges them to seek help with the process.

Visit ramblingdogpublications.com for some suggested resources on pet grief.